Looking at . . . Ouranosaurus

A Dinosaur from the CRETACEOUS Period

Weekly Reader® BOOKS

Published by arrangement with Gareth Stevens, Inc.
Newfield Publications is a federally registered trademark
of Newfield Publications, Inc. Weekly Reader is a federally
registered trademark of Weekly Reader Corporation.

Library of Congress Cataloging-in-Publication Data

Freedman, Frances.
    Looking at— Ouranosaurus / written by Frances Freedman; illustrated by Tony Gibbons. —
North American ed.
      p. cm. — (The new dinosaur collection)
    ISBN 0-8368-1276-X
    1. Ouranosaurus—Juvenile literature. [1. Ouranosaurus.] I. Gibbons, Tony, ill. II. Title.
III. Title: Ouranosaurus. IV. Series.
QE862.065F737 1995
567.9'7—dc20   94-36067

This North American edition first published in 1995 by
Gareth Stevens Publishing
1555 North RiverCenter Drive, Suite 201
Milwaukee, Wisconsin 53212 USA

This U.S. edition © 1995 by Gareth Stevens, Inc. Created with original © 1994 by Quartz
Editorial Services, Premier House, 112 Station Road, Edgware HA8 7AQ U.K.

Consultant: Dr. David Norman, Director of the Sedgwick Museum of Geology,
University of Cambridge, England.

Additional artwork by Clare Herronneau.

Printed in the United States of America

Weekly Reader Books Presents

Looking at . . . Ouranosaurus

A Dinosaur from the CRETACEOUS Period

by Frances Freedman

Illustrated by Tony Gibbons

THE NEW
DINOSAUR
COLLECTION

Gareth Stevens Publishing
MILWAUKEE

Contents

Introducing
Ouranosaurus

Join us as we begin a journey back to Cretaceous times — over 100 million years ago, long before human beings even existed.

What a large animal it was!

When it stood on its hind legs, this strange-looking dinosaur was about twice the height of a fully grown human. It also had what looked like a large sail running down its back.

What was this sail for? And how did **Ouranosaurus** spend its prehistoric day? Find the answers to these and many other

Earth was very different then. If you had been alive at that time, living in the area of the world we now know as western Africa, you might have come face-to-face with an **Ouranosaurus** (OO-<u>RAN</u>-OH-<u>SAW</u>-RUS).

questions about this amazing creature on the following pages.

Dinosaur from

What an amazing sight! A massive dinosaur, 23 feet (7 meters) long from the tip of its snout to the end of its tail, with a bizarre

structure that looked like a sail rising from its back! Would it attack, or was it friendly?

6

the Sahara

First discovered in the Sahara Desert in 1966, remains of **Ouranosaurus** show it was a heavy creature with strong back legs and shorter front limbs.

It was a plant-eater and quite a peaceful animal unless provoked. It probably needed the claws at the end of its fingers, as well as its spiked thumb, for self-defense.

Ouranosaurus had a flexible neck it could move easily. This helped it gather food and stay alert for danger.

If meat-eating enemies were around, **Ouranosaurus** would have had to live up to its name, which means "brave reptile."

Look carefully at the drawing shown here, and you can see that underneath the skin covering the sail on **Ouranosaurus**'s back was a row of tall spines.

Take a good look at **Ouranosaurus**'s head, too. What an odd shape it was! And what large nostrils it had! The snout was broad and flat at the end of long jaws. There were no teeth at the front of its mouth, but it had closely-packed cheek teeth for grinding vegetation.

Spectacular

After a team of French scientists led by Dr. Philippe Taquet dug up the almost complete skeleton of an **Ouranosaurus** in 1966, they soon noticed how it looked like **Iguanodon** (IG-WA-NO-DON). Both were large, strong creatures. Both also had spiked thumbs as weapons.

Iguanodon and **Ouranosaurus** both had three-toed feet. Both dinosaurs had powerful front limbs, too, on which they may have rested or walked at times.

It would not have been very difficult to spot the differences between them, however.

Ouranosaurus had something very special — the large spines on its back.

skeleton

These spines, as paleontologists have guessed, must have been covered with skin to form what looked like a sail. See if you can count the spines in the drawing of the **Ouranosaurus** skeleton shown here. What a lot there were!

Ouranosaurus was an ornithopod (OR-<u>NITH</u>-THOE-POD) dinosaur. This means it was a herbivore, eating plants only and no meat, and it had what scientists call "bird-hips." In bird-hipped dinosaurs, the pubis bone points backward, at the hips. Can you spot it?

In other types of dinosaurs, this bone points forward. (Did you know some scientists believe birds evolved from dinosaurs?)

Turn the page to find out more about **Ouranosaurus**'s mysterious sail.

Keeping cool, keeping warm

At first, scientists were puzzled about the purpose of that strange sail on **Ouranosaurus**'s back.

But they believe the most likely explanation is that it was used as a heating and cooling system. Just as solar panels on buildings are used to take in heat from the sun, so blood in the sail's skin would be warmed up by the sun on a cool morning. Later, in the hot Cretaceous day, the sail could help keep **Ouranosaurus** cool by releasing heat.

Ouranosaurus's day

Ouranosaurus awoke slowly and shivered a little. Cretaceous nights were chilly, but it would soon warm up as the sail on its back

It was still early, and the world's first flowering plants were just opening up to greet the light.

absorbed the heat from prehistoric Africa's morning sun.

The night had passed without disturbance. Other creatures, too, were now rising.

Ouranosaurus was hungry and lumbered along to search for fresh leaves and twigs for breakfast. The vegetation was still damp with dew and wonderfully refreshing.

What a delicious meal for a herbivore!

Ssh! What was that? What had started as a distant running sound now grew louder.

Fortunately, the noise was familiar, and there was no need for **Ouranosaurus** to panic. It was simply a herd of ostrichlike dinosaurs that would not attack. Instead, they were probably

just looking for new feeding grounds.

They, too, were herbivores and not interested in having a meal of raw dinosaur flesh.

Ouranosaurus went back to peacefully munching on crisp vegetation when, suddenly, out rushed three **Inosaurus** (<u>IN</u>-OH-<u>SAW</u>-RUS). Although half **Ouranosaurus**'s size, they were nasty predators when hungry. **Ouranosaurus** would make a delicious meal.

Ouranosaurus roared as the **Inosaurus** attacked. Then **Ouranosaurus** savagely dug its thumb spike deep into the flesh of

one of the carnivores. The **Inosaurus** squealed in pain and collapsed. The other two **Inosaurus** took warning and fled.

13

African discoveries

Some of the most interesting dinosaurs of all have been found on the African continent — everywhere from Algeria in the north, and Nigeria in the west, to Zimbabwe and South Africa in the south. Let's visit Africa and find out which dinosaur skeletons have been discovered.

Ouranosaurus (**1**) lived in what is now the Sahara Desert. There, in the country of Niger, many **Ouranosaurus** bones were found on the surface of the ground because the wind had blown away layers of sand.

Iguanodon's bones (**2**) have been unearthed in Tunisia; and Niger again, as well as Egypt, was home to another sail-backed dinosaur, **Spinosaurus** (SPINE-O-SAW-RUS) (**3**).

In Zimbabwe and Tanzania, paleontologists found the remains of huge, long-necked **Brachiosaurus** (BRACK-EE-OH-SAW-RUS) (**4**).

Many African countries — South Africa, Lesotho, Malawi, Morocco, and Nigeria — have what scientists call "dinosaur beds," too. These are large areas with lots of dinosaur remains. These include the long-legged plant-eater **Lesothosaurus** (LESS-OH-TOE-SAW-RUS) (**5**), found in Lesotho; the big carnivore **Carcharodontosaurus** (CAR-CAR-O-DONT-OH-SAW-RUS) (**6**), from northern Africa; **Kentrosaurus**, (KEN-TRO-SAW-RUS) (**7**), with its plated back and tail spines, from Tanzania; and **Vulcanodon** (VUL-KAN-OH-DON) (**8**), found without its neck and head so scientists had to guess what it must have looked

like from the rest of
its skeleton.

Other dinosaurs from
Africa include little
Syntarsus (SIN-<u>TAR</u>-SUS) **(9)**,
found in Zimbabwe and
South Africa; and
Massospondylus (<u>MASS</u>-
OH-<u>SPOND</u>-IH-LUS) **(10)**, a
Triassic plant-eater also
from southern Africa.

15

The great

dragon myth

When paleontologists first dug up dinosaur skeletons in the nineteenth century, everyone found it hard to believe such wonderful creatures ever existed.

But the ancient Chinese had, in fact, found dinosaur remains a long time before this — about two thousand years ago. They used to call them "dragon bones" or "dragon teeth."

An **Ouranosaurus** may have resembled a winged dragon in some ways, as you can see here. But now, of course, we know dinosaurs did indeed rule this planet for hundreds of millions of years before humankind. Fire-breathing dragons, though, belong only in storybooks.

On two feet or four?

How did **Ouranosaurus** move around? Scientists think it walked either on just its two back legs or on all fours.

The back legs were sturdy enough to support its weight. But **Ouranosaurus** (1) might have used its front limbs to help keep its balance when it needed a rest— much like today's kangaroos — and may even have walked using the front limbs, too.

Some dinosaurs — 82-foot (25-m)-long **Brachiosaurus** (2), for example — usually walked on all fours but would rear up on their hind legs to eat leaves at the top of the tallest trees. **Stegosaurus** (3), too, with the amazing two rows of plates along its back, and three-horned **Triceratops** (TRY-<u>SER</u>-A-TOPS) (4) moved around on four strong legs.

Bipedal dinosaurs — those that used only two legs to get around — include the fearsome predator **Tyrannosaurus rex** (TIE-RANN-OH-SAW-RUS-RECKS) **(6)**, the small carnivore **Coelophysis** (SEEL-OH-FY-SIS) **(7)**, and plant-eating **Psittacosaurus** (SI-TAK-OH-SAW-RUS) **(8)**. These three dinosaurs all look different, but what they had in common was walking on just two feet.

Baryonyx (BAR-EE-ON-IX) **(5)**, known for a thumb claw scientists believe was used for fishing, is another dinosaur that could probably choose between walking on just its back legs or on all four limbs.

19

Ouranosaurus data

Let's go on an **Ouranosaurus** hunt! If you had been around when **Ouranosaurus** lived, you would have been able to recognize one by the following features. But there would have been no need to be scared. It was a herbivore, which means it ate plants only and would not have attacked you for its dinner.

Magnificent sail

What made **Ouranosaurus** special was the splendid sail on its back. It probably had lots of blood vessels in this part of its body. Remains of **Ouranosaurus** have been found in parts of the world that were very hot and dry by day, and perhaps colder by night. Scientists think this sail may have worked like a solar panel, taking heat from the morning sun into its blood vessels to keep warm.

Big head

You would have needed to look closely at its head, too. By dinosaur standards, **Ouranosaurus** had a fairly large head. Its jaws were long and powerful, while its snout was broad and flat. The inside of its mouth had lots of ridged cheek teeth. The neck was flexible and moved easily from side to side.

Sturdy legs

When **Ouranosaurus**-spotting, you would also have needed to watch for legs that looked like pillars. **Ouranosaurus** was not a fast runner, and it had just three toes at the end of its short feet.

Handy hands

The claws on **Ouranosaurus**'s fingers were hooflike and useful for walking, if it wanted to move on all fours. And, of course, it had thumb spikes — nasty weapons with which to strike its enemies. **Ouranosaurus** probably used its longer fingers to grab plants to eat.

Scaly skin

No one knows for sure what color **Ouranosaurus** was; our illustrator has had to guess. But chances are its skin was tough and scaly, a little like a crocodile's.

Dinosaurs with heating systems

By now, you should be able to recognize an **Ouranosaurus** (**1**) if you spot one in a book or when visiting a museum. The sail is the main clue. But other dinosaurs, too, had strangely formed backs that helped control their body temperature.

Acrocanthosaurus
(<u>ACK</u>-ROE-<u>CAN</u>-THO-<u>SAW</u>-RUS) (**2**), for example, also from Cretaceous times, lived in what is now Oklahoma. Its name means "very spiny reptile." It was about 40 feet (12 m) long and had a slightly raised sail-like ridge along its back.

But the back sail of the 40-foot (12-m)-long, meat-eating African dinosaur **Spinosaurus** (SPY-NOE-SAW-RUS) (**3**), was much larger.

Metriacanthosaurus (MET-REE-AH-CAN-THO-SAW-RUS) (**4**), with a name meaning "long spined lizard," lived in Early Jurassic times, 130 million years ago, in what is now southern England. This 26-foot (8-m)-long predator also had long back spines.

Stegosaurus (STEG-OH-SAW-RUS) (**5**) from Jurassic North America had two rows of plates on its back to use as a heating system.

How super-efficient these creatures must have been with these built-in temperature control units!

3

4

5

GLOSSARY

carnivores — meat-eating animals.

continents — the major landmasses of Earth. Europe, Asia, Africa, Australia, North America, South America, and Antarctica are continents.

evolve — to change shape or develop gradually over a long period of time.

herbivores — plant-eating animals.

herd — a group of animals that travels together.

massive — very large and heavy.

paleontologists — scientists who study the remains of plants and animals that lived millions of years ago.

predators — animals that capture and kill other animals for food.

remains — a skeleton, bones, or a dead body.

reptiles — cold-blooded animals that have hornlike or scale-covered skin.

INDEX